# Origami

## Activities for Children

# by Chiyo Araki

**TUTTLE** Publishing

Tokyo | Rutland, Vermont | Singapore

# Contents

Published by Tuttle Publishing,
an imprint of Periplus Editions (HK) Ltd.

**www.tuttlepublishing.com**

© 1968, 2002 by Charles E. Tuttle Co.

All rights reserved

LCC Card No. 2002103226
ISBN 978-0-8048-3311-0

Published in 1968
Second edition 2002

15  14  13  12  11        1107CP
11  10  9  8  7  6

Printed in Singapore

# Introduction

Origami—the art of paper folding—has a long history in Japan and is one of the major crafts in the country. It is believed that the people of Japan first started making paper models during the 8th century, in the Heinan period, in connection with the Hina Matsuri or Doll Festival, which was observed every year on 3 March. On this day, children were said to have made dolls out of paper which were later thrown into a river. They believed that as the dolls were swept away in the river, the evil spirits which lurked within the bodies of the children were also swept away.

As time passed, the art of paper folding became more and more popular, and it also developed at different stages. Originally, there were two styles of making origami—a formal style known as *gishi-ki*, and an informal style called *shumi-no-origami*. Paper models made in the formal style were used as gifts and gift decorations and for display during shrine and temple festivals. Figures made in the less formal style were enjoyed largely as a hobby. Today, origami is made in a variety of styles for many different reasons.

Most Japanese have been brought up on the art of origami since they were very young. Thus, there are many people in Japan who are very skilled in origami, but even those with a passing interest in it are able to develop new designs and folding techniques. Some professional artists are able to incorporate modern-day themes into magnificent and complicated works. Because of the great interest in origami, many exhibits are held in Japan every year.

Origami can be enjoyed by people of all ages. It is particularly suitable for young children in the classroom and at home. Not only does it develop their creativity and imagination, but it also develops coordination and logic and allows them to participate in a variety of artistic activities. The children may fold, cut, paste, draw and tie, and then use what they have made in their play. Through the use of crayon, pastel and water paint, they can practice the many techniques required in drawing.

Children also become acquainted with geometric figures such as the triangle and the square. Origami requires precision. It is impossible to skip a step. An origami figure cannot be made unless the flat paper is folded with much care, step by step, along the correct folding lines. Practice is the most important requirement.

In this book, I have included origami projects which are relevant to events and holidays in the US and other Western countries, through all seasons, as these are always important in the lives of children. The book provides training in the fundamentals of paper folding. Beginning with one square sheet of paper, the steps are explained in detail. Diagrams illustrate each step, and a full-color photograph shows each finished origami model.

I have also suggested grade levels for each project, as well as the time it will take to make each model, and the materials that are needed. However, children should be encouraged to improvise with whatever materials are available, and to attempt models at different grades.

My wish is that children will enjoy this little book, and that it will become a friend and guide to a new art medium. It has been my privilege to introduce a small part of Japanese culture and an easily mastered art.

CHIYO ARAKI

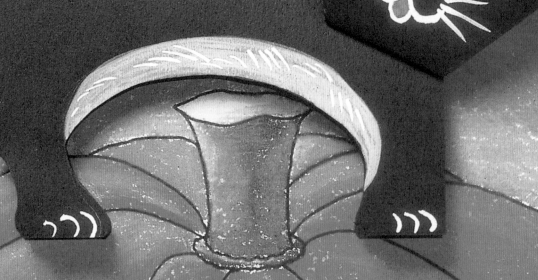

HALLOWEEN

# Pussy Cat

**Level:** Middle grades
**Time:** 1½ hours
**Materials:** Folding paper: white (6" x 6") for face
Construction paper:
• Orange (18" x 1") for body
• Black (18" x 1") for body
• Orange (4½" x ½") two pieces for arms
• Black (9" x 1") for legs

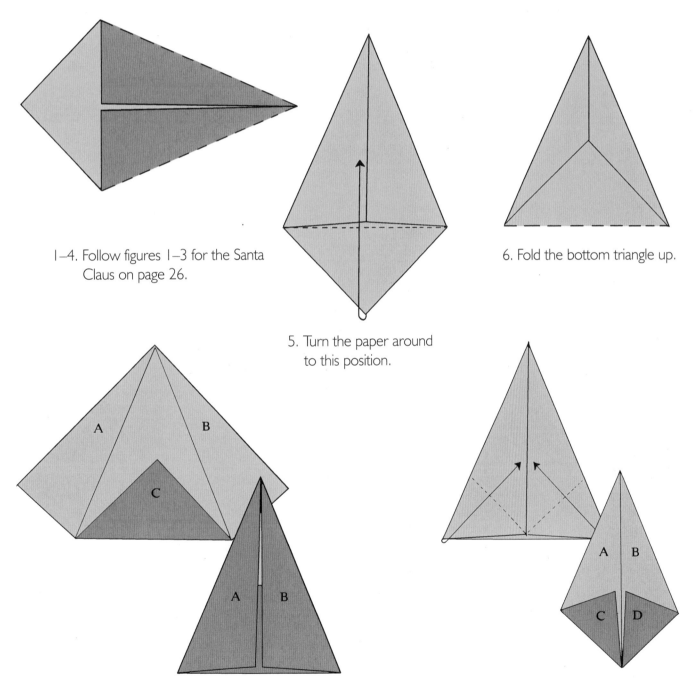

1–4. Follow figures 1–3 for the Santa Claus on page 26.

6. Fold the bottom triangle up.

5. Turn the paper around to this position.

7–8. Open A, B and C and slip C under A and B.

9–10. Fold the left and right side points to the center line.

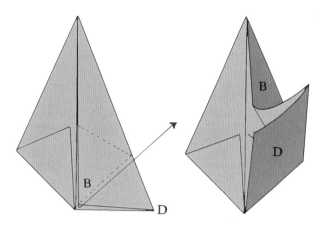

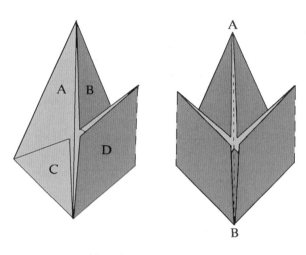

11–12. Bring the folded flap B from under D and flatten it to form a diamond shape.

13–14. Repeat with C.

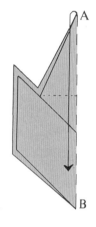

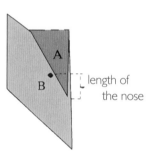

15. Turn over and fold the paper in half along the straight line AB.

16. Bring point A down. For the length of the nose, mark point B by the edge of triangle A.

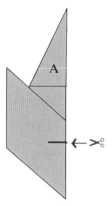

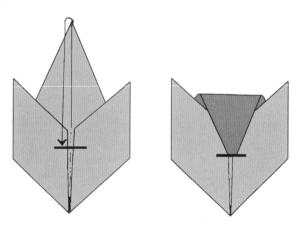

17. Open A and draw a horizontal line from the mark to the right edge and then cut along this line.

18–19. Unfold the center fold and slip the top point through the opening.

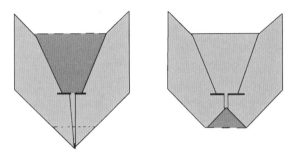

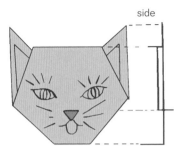
side

20–21. Fold up a little of the bottom point.

22. Turn the paper over and stand the nose up. Make the eyes, mouth, whiskers and tongue with scraps of colored construction paper.

## BODY

1. Paste the end of the orange paper across the end of the black paper.

2. Bring the black paper over the orange. Do not leave space between the orange and the black.

3. Bring the orange over the black. Repeat this to the end of the paper and paste the ends.

4. Paste the head onto the body. Paste the arms under the neck, and paste the legs to the bottom.

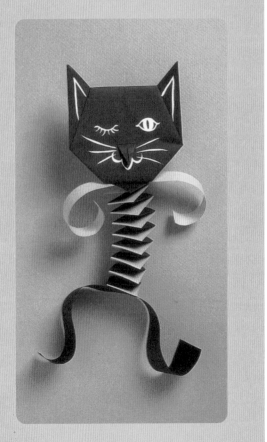

# Bat

**Level:** Lower grades
**Time:** 45 minutes
**Materials:** Folding paper: black (6" x 6")
Construction paper (12" x 9") for drawing scenery
Color crayons or water paint, scissors and paste

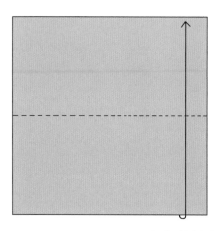

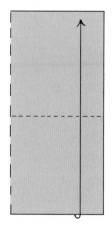

1–2. Fold the paper in half.

3. Fold in half the other way.

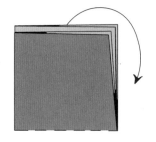

4. Turn the paper on its side as shown.

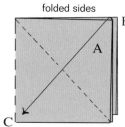

folded sides

5–6. Bring A to C and crease.

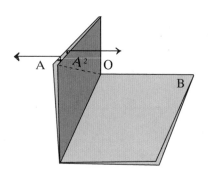

7. Bring folded A up straight and open A and A².

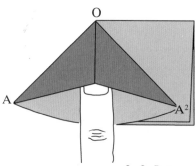

8–9. Put your finger into O and fold the flap down to form a triangle with O, A and A².

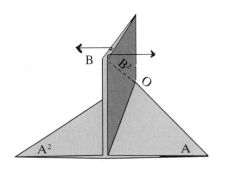

10. Turn over and repeat, lifting up the square corner and then opening it.

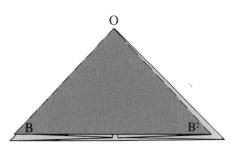

11. Bring B² over to B.

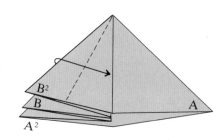

12. Fold B² in half.

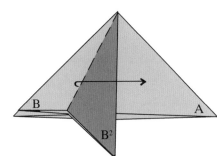

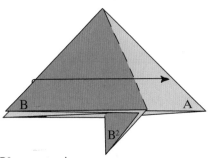

13–14. Bring folded B² over to A.

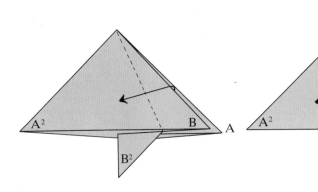

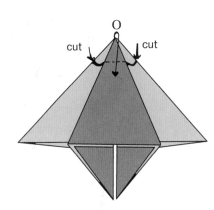

15–16. Repeat with side B.

17. Cut along the lines for the ears and fold point O down to the front.

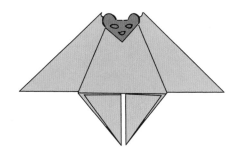

18. Make the eyes and mouth.

# Cat for a Halloween Lantern

**Level:** Lower grades
**Time:** 45 minutes
**Materials:** Folding paper (6" x 6") two pieces
Construction paper (12" x 9")
Crayons or water paint, paste and scissors

**FACE**

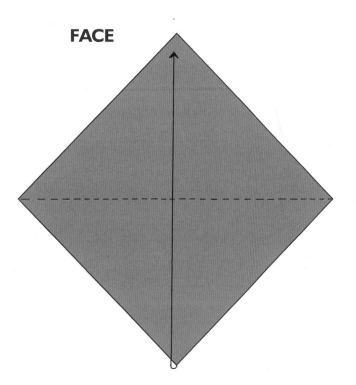

1. Fold the paper into a triangle.

2. Bring point A to point B and find point C on line AB and then reopen. Bring point B to the left, folding at mark C.

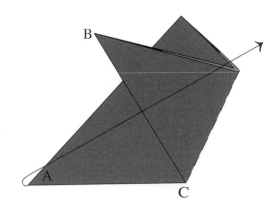

3. Bring point A to the right.

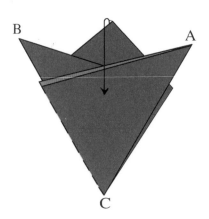

4. Fold the top down.

10

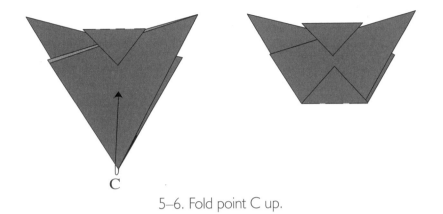

5–6. Fold point C up.

7. Turn over. Make the face with scraps of colored paper.

## BODY

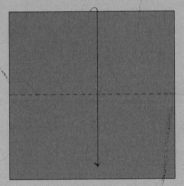

1. Fold the paper in half.

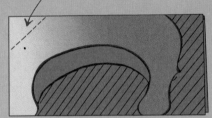

Paste face here

2. Draw the body and tail, cut them out, and then paste the face on where indicated.

<table>
<tr><td>Level:</td><td>Middle grades</td></tr>
<tr><td>Time:</td><td>1 1/2 hours</td></tr>
<tr><td>Materials:</td><td>Folding paper: orange (6" × 6") for face</td></tr>
</table>

# Jack o'Lantern

**Level:** Middle grades
**Time:** 1 ½ hours
**Materials:** Folding paper: orange (6" × 6") for face
Construction paper:
- Green (5" × ¼" or ½") 4 pieces for arms and legs
- Green (6" × 5") for leaf hat
- Orange (2" × 2") for hands and feet
Thread of any color (7"), toothpick, bamboo stick or branch

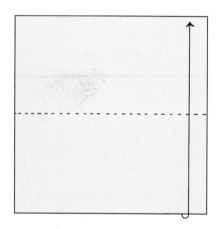

1. Fold the paper in half.

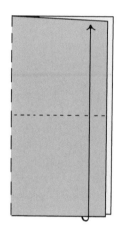

2. Fold in half again.

folded sides

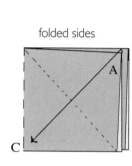

3–4. Bring A to C and crease.

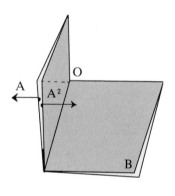

5. Hold A up straight and open A and A².

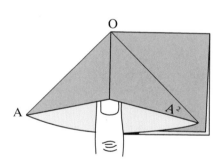

6. Put your finger inside to top O and press the flap down to form triangle O, A and A².

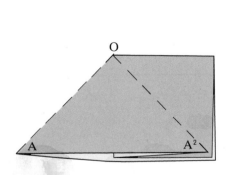

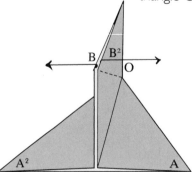

7–8. Turn over and repeat.

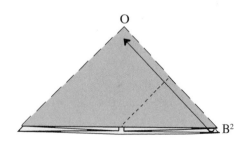

9. Bring B² to top O.

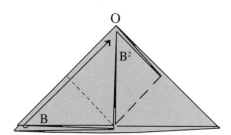

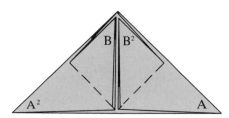

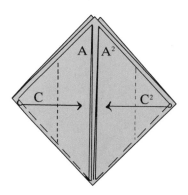

10. Repeat with side B.

11. Turn over and repeat with A and $A^2$.

12. Turn the paper around and bring C and $C^2$ to the center line.

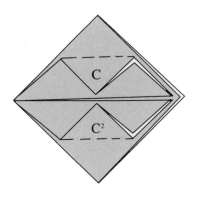

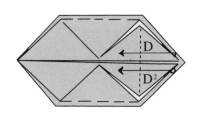

13. Turn over and repeat.

14. Fold triangle D and $D^2$ to the left.

15. Fold D and $D^2$ over into the pockets of the C and $C^2$ triangles.

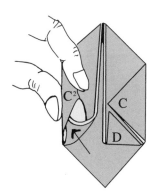

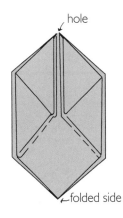

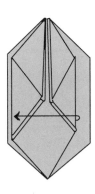

16. To do this, open the triangle pockets with your fingers and slip the edge in.

17. Turn over and repeat on the same end.

18. Close the right side to the left so that the plain side is showing.

hole

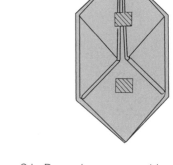

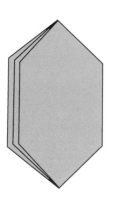

19. Turn over and repeat.

20. Draw the face between the dotted lines indicated.

21. Paste the arms and legs on both sides at the places marked. Blow through the hole carefully.

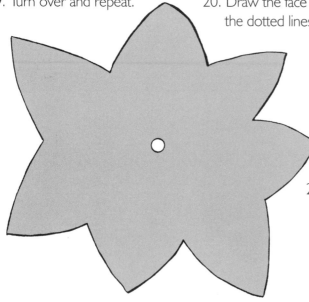

22. Trace the leaf pattern and cut it out of green paper.

## ARMS AND LEGS

5"

1/4"
or
1/2"

For the arms and legs, take four pieces of paper and make accordion folds along the length of each strip.

## HANDS AND FEET

To make the hands, fold the orange paper (2" square) in half and then in half again. Draw one hand on the top and cut around it through all layers.

## HANGING THE JACK O'LANTERN

Tie one end of the thread to a toothpick. Pull the other end of the thread through the hole in the leaf. Tie the thread to a bamboo stick very tightly. Slip the toothpick into the hole in the top of the Jack o'Lantern.

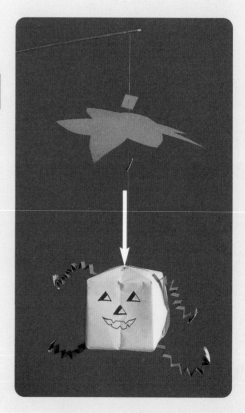

# Party Baskets

# Basket A

**Level:** All grades
**Time:** 20–40 minutes
**Materials:** Folding paper (6" x 6", or desired size)

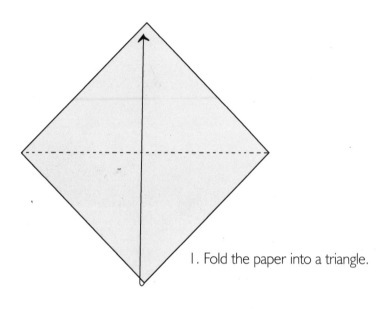

1. Fold the paper into a triangle.

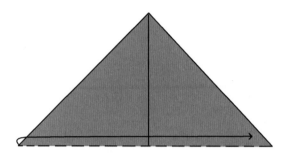

2. Fold into a triangle again.

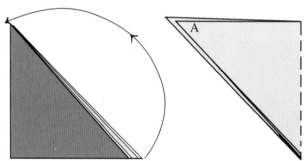

3–4. Turn the paper around.

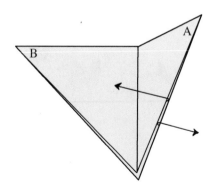

5. Hold A up straight.

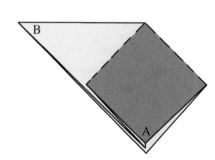

6. Open the left and right sides and press down in a diamond.

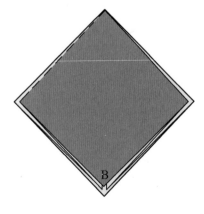

7. Turn over and repeat with B, holding the long tip up straight and opening it into a diamond.

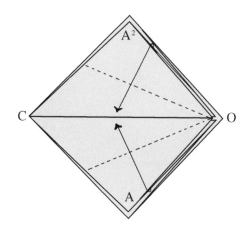

8. Turn the paper on its side.

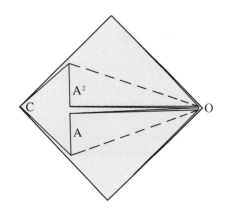

9. Bring A and A² to the CO line so it looks like this.

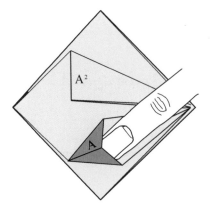

10. Open A with your finger and press it down. Repeat with A².

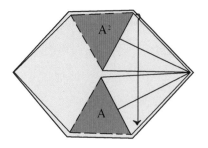

11. Bring A² over to A.

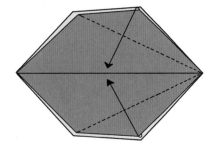

12. Turn over and repeat.

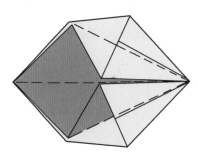

13. You can see three creased lines. Bring both sides to the center crease. Turn over and repeat.

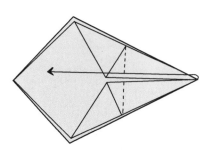

14. Bring one of the points all the way to the left. Turn over and repeat.

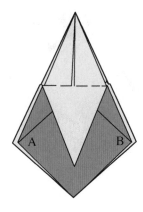

15. Bring the top flap A to the opposite side B and fold down the point.

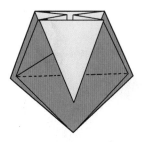

16. Turn over and repeat so that it looks like this. The dotted line indicated is to be the bottom.

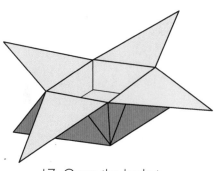

17. Open the basket.

# Basket B

**Level:** Upper grades
**Time:** 30 minutes
**Materials:** Folding paper (6" x 6", or desired size)

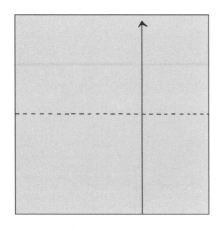

1. Fold the paper in half.

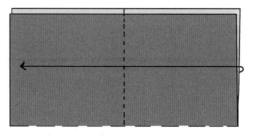

2–3. Fold in half again.

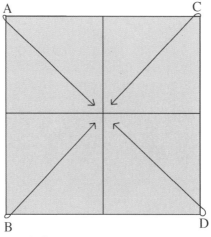

4. Open so you can see the creased lines.

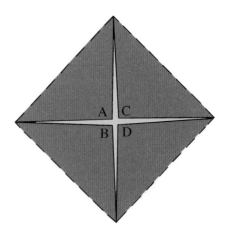

5. Bring points A, B, C and D to the center.

6. Turn over and fold the paper in half.

7. Fold in half again.

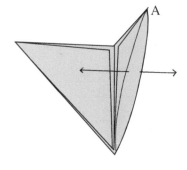

8. Hold side A up straight.

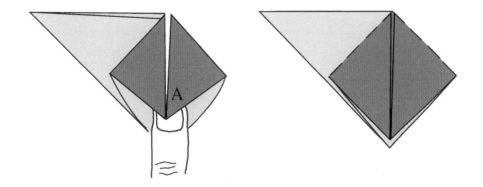

9–10. Open side A into a diamond. Turn over and repeat, holding the long tip up straight and then opening it into a diamond.

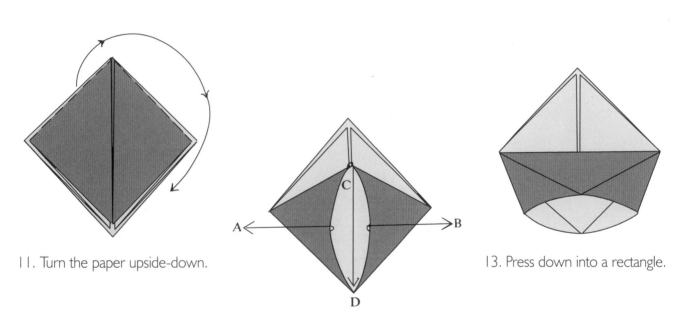

11. Turn the paper upside-down.

12. Open the front paper A and B to the left and right. Bring down point C to D.

13. Press down into a rectangle.

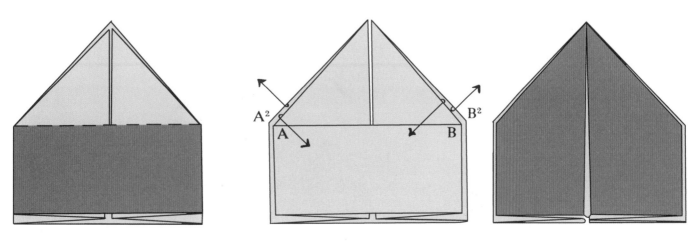

14. Turn it over and repeat.

15–16. Open sides A and A², B and B².

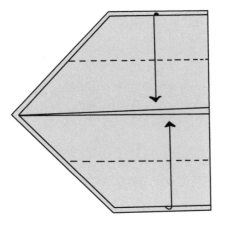

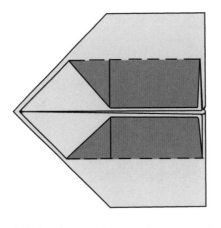

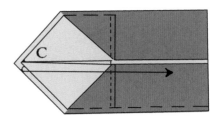

17. Turn the paper on its side.

18. Bring both edges to the center line.

19–20. Bring C to the right.

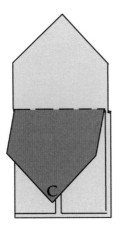

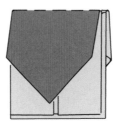

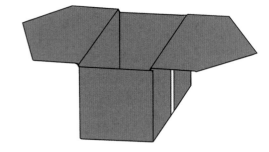

21. Turn over and repeat.

22. Open the basket.

SEASON'S GREETINGS

Christmas

happy holidays

# Church

**Level:** Middle grades
**Time:** 1 hour
**Materials:** Folding paper: black (12" x 12", or desired size)
Construction paper:
- White (12" x 9")
- Green (12" x 9")
- Brown scraps

Color crayons or water paint, scissors and paste

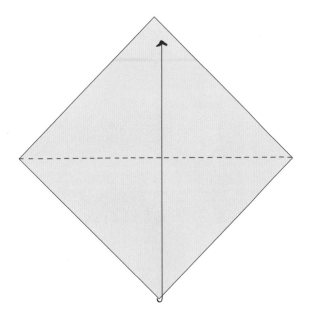

1. Fold the paper into a triangle.

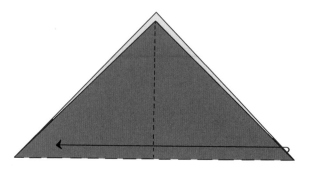

2. Fold into a triangle again.

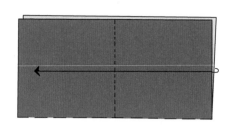

3. Crease the triangle well.

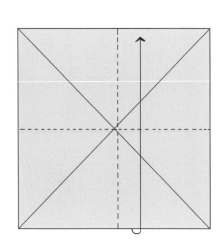

4. Open the paper so you can see the diagonal lines.

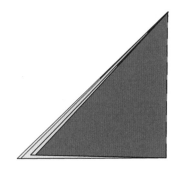

5. Fold it in half twice.

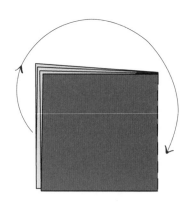

6. Turn it around.

7. Hold A straight up.

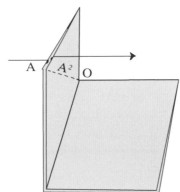

8–9. Open A and $A^2$ by putting your finger inside to top O. Fold into a triangle.

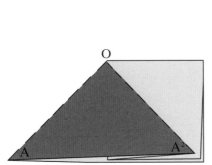

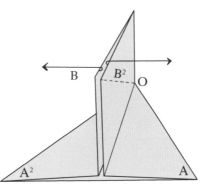

10–11. Turn over and repeat, holding the corner up straight and then opening into a triangle.

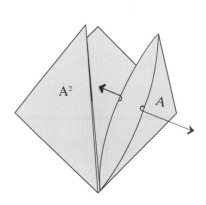

12–13. Bring points B and $B^2$ to the top O.

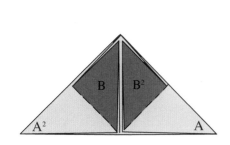

14. Turn over and repeat with A and $A^2$.

15. Pull side A out.

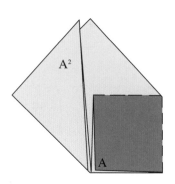

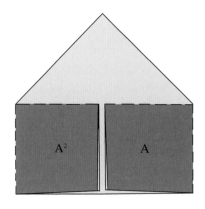

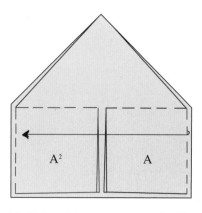

16. Press down into a square.

17. Repeat with side $A^2$. Turn over and repeat with the other two points.

18. Bring side A over to side $A^2$.

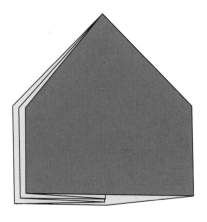

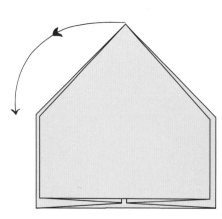

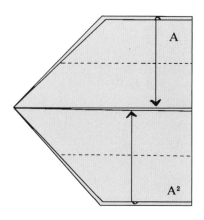

19. Turn over and repeat on the other side.

20. Turn the paper on its side.

21–22. Bring sides A and $A^2$ to the creased line in the center. Turn over and repeat on the other side.

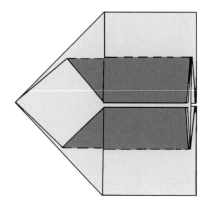

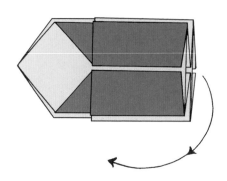

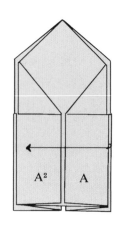

23. Turn the paper around.

24–25. Bring side A over to side $A^2$.

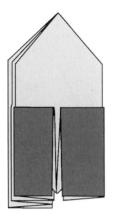

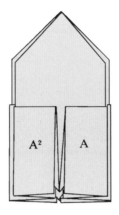

26. Turn over and repeat.

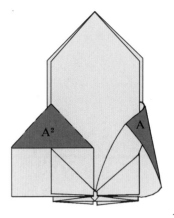

27. Open side A² and press it down flat to form the roof shape. Repeat with side A.

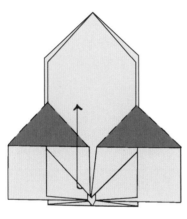

28. Bring the triangle which points to the center of the bottom up and fold it back.

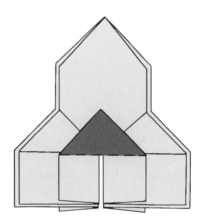

29. Turn over and repeat. Draw the doors, windows and bell. Cut out a cross and paste it on the top.

## TREES

Cut out two trees. Slit one halfway down the center and the other halfway up. Fit the two trees together and adjust them so that they can stand up by themselves.

The church will look more attractive if you make two Christmas trees out of green construction paper and place them on either side.

# Santa Claus

**Level:** Lower grades
**Time:** 1 hour
**Materials:** Folding paper: red (6" x 6") two pieces
Construction paper:
- White (two circles, one 7" and the other 1½" in diameter)
- Blue (12" x 9")
- Green, red and yellow scraps

## BODY

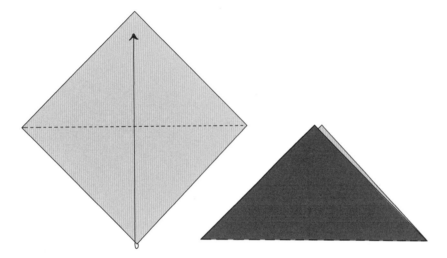

1–2. Fold the paper into a triangle.

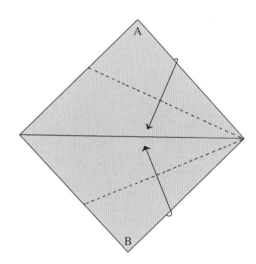

3. Unfold and bring A and B to the creased center line.

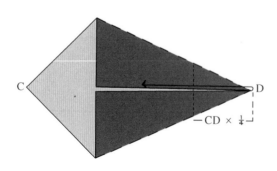

4. Fold D to the left a quarter the length of CD.

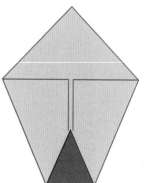

5–6. Turn the paper over.

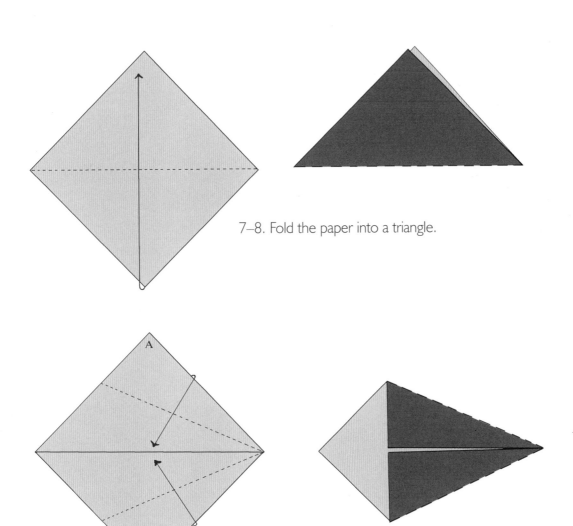

7–8. Fold the paper into a triangle.

9–10. Unfold and bring A and B to the creased line in the center.

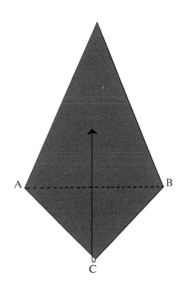

11. Turn over.

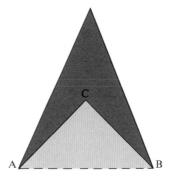

12. Fold triangle ABC back. Open the last fold.

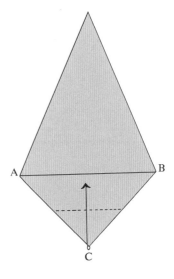

13. Bring point C straight up to crease line AB.

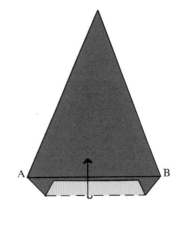
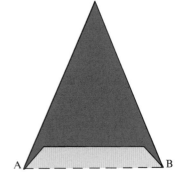

14. Bring the bottom up to line AB.

15–16. Fold at line AB, bringing the bottom up.

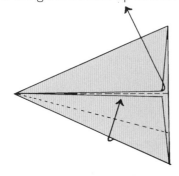
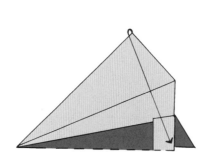
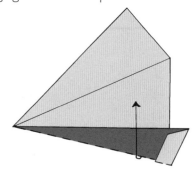

17. Turn over and bring the bottom slanting edge to the creased line in the center.

18. Bring the opened point to the opposite bottom corner.

19. Open the top side out flat. Fold the lower side over again.

**FACE**

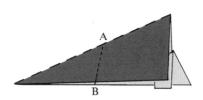

20. Fold along line AB.

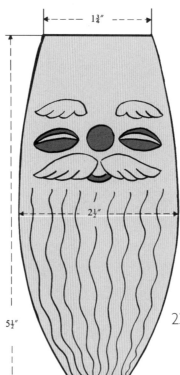

1¾″

2½″

5½″

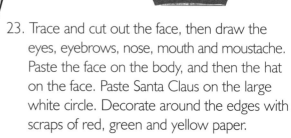

21–22. Turn over. Paste the 2½" diameter white circle on the end of the hat.

23. Trace and cut out the face, then draw the eyes, eyebrows, nose, mouth and moustache. Paste the face on the body, and then the hat on the face. Paste Santa Claus on the large white circle. Decorate around the edges with scraps of red, green and yellow paper.

# Penguin

**Level:** Middle grades
**Time:** 40 minutes
**Materials:** Folding paper: black (6" x 6"). Japanese origami paper is colored on one side and white on the other. If you use plain white or black paper, color the penguin when you have finished.
Orange scraps (1" x 1½") for feet
Paste, scissors, crayons or paint

Begin with the black side up when using Japanese origami paper.

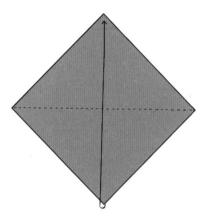

1. Fold the paper in half.

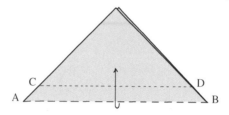

2. Fold up about ½" along the dotted CD line.

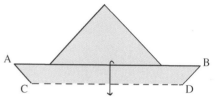

3. Unfold the bottom AB and you will see the folded CD line.

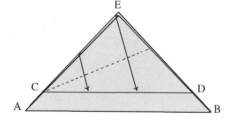

4. Fold the top part CE down on the dotted line along the CD line.

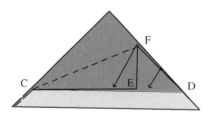

5. Fold the FD part down along the CD line.

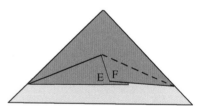

6. Turn the paper over and repeat steps 4–5.

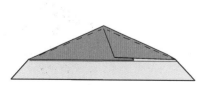

7. Your paper should look like this.

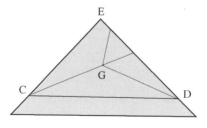

8–9. Unfold one side only. See the fold lines. Turn the paper as in diagram 9. Bend the paper in half.

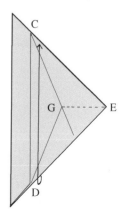

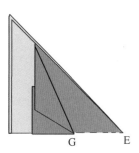

10. Press down from G to E only. Crease GE well, and then open.

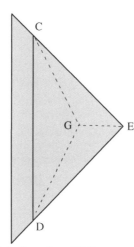

11. See the GE line.

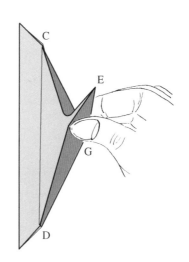

12. Hold the folded GE part (black) from the outside with the thumb and index finger. Crease the CG and GD lines well. Point E stands up.

13. Bring point E down toward D.

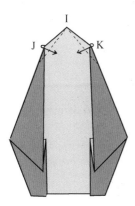

14–15. Turn the paper over and repeat steps 7–14. Make sure points E and F are folded in the same direction.

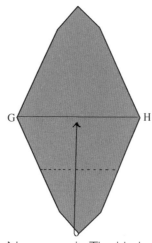

16. Now open it. The black side should be face up. Fold the bottom point up to GH.

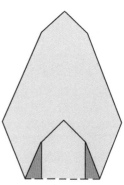

17. Crease the folded part well. Turn the paper over.

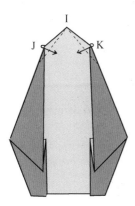

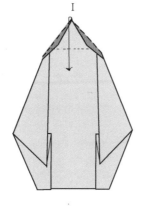

18–19. Point I will be the head. Fold under corners J and K, slanting them a little to make the head pointed. Fold point I down about 1".

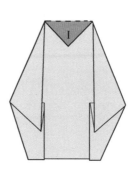

20. Turn the paper over.

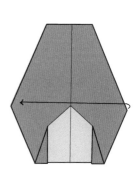

21. Fold the paper in half from right to left lengthwise. Crease the folded part well.

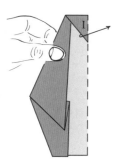 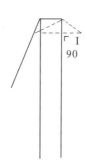

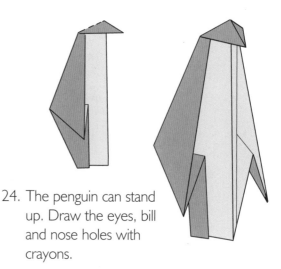

22–23. Hold the wings close to the head with the thumb and index finger. Pull the point I part out as the diagram shows. Crease the folded head well. Open the penguin.

24. The penguin can stand up. Draw the eyes, bill and nose holes with crayons.

## FEET

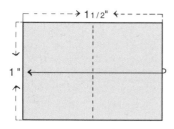 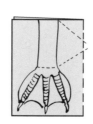

Paste this part on the back of the penguin.

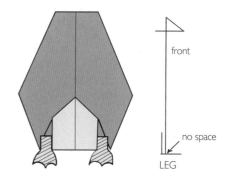

front

no space

LEG

25. Fold the orange construction paper in half. Draw the feet and cut them out. The size and location of the feet are important.

26. Paste the feet on the back of the penguin. The feet should be pasted on the edges of the black paper as shown. Fold the feet out in front of the penguin.

## USING BLACK CONSTRUCTION PAPER

When you have learned how to fold a penguin with folding paper, try making one with black (12" x 12") construction paper. You can make a penguin about 10" high with this size paper. You will need orange scraps (2$\frac{1}{2}$" x 4") for the feet, and white drawing paper (9" x 3$\frac{1}{2}$") for the breast of the penguin.

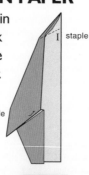

staple

staple

Fold the penguin following the steps in diagrams 1–17. Fold the white paper in half lengthwise, then open it. Put a little paste on the edges. Slip it on the body for the breast, and staple under the head. Then go back to diagram 18. When finished, paste or staple the wings and neck together. Make the feet and paste them on behind the white part.

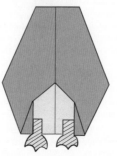

# Box with Valentine

**Level:** Middle and upper grades
**Time:** 1 hour
**Materials:** Folding paper: red, white or old magazine (8" x 8")
for cover; 7³/₄" x 7³/₄" for bottom of box.
For each smaller box, use a ¹/₄" smaller square of paper.
Writing paper: white or pink (4" x 4") for a small valentine
Scissors and paste
It is possible to teach younger children this box if you pre-cut the paper to the desired size.

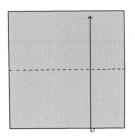

1. Fold in half.

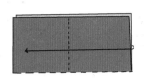

2–3. Fold in half again and then unfold.

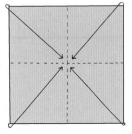

4. Fold the four corners to the center.

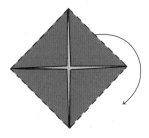

5. Turn the paper.

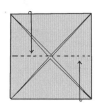

6. Fold the bottom and top to the center line.

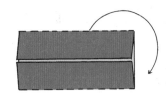

7. Turn.

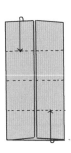

8. Fold the bottom and top to the center line.

9. Crease well and unfold back to step 5.

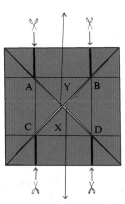

10–11. Cut on the indicated points A, B, C and D. Open parts Y and X.

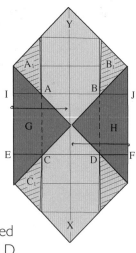

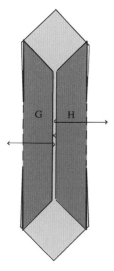

12. Fold sides G and H on the dotted lines. Crease well and open.

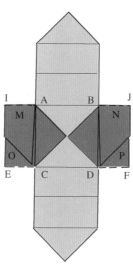

13. Fold parts M, N, O and P on the IA, BJ, EC and DF lines. Crease well.

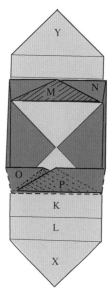

14. Open and put the shaded triangles O and P together. Hold tightly.

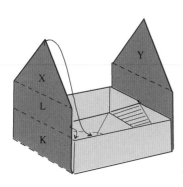

15. Cover outside O and P with K, inside O and P with L. Crease well. The triangle X fits the bottom. Repeat steps 14–15 with the other side.

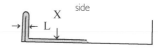

16. Make another box using 7³⁄₄" x 7³⁄₄" paper. The first box may be used as the cover.

## VALENTINE GIFTS

Make a valentine and paste it on top of the box. Include a little gift in the box.

1. Fold a 4" x 4" square of paper (pink, white or red) in half, then in half again.
2. Draw a valentine on it as shown, and cut out.
3. Open and write a greeting.

Make a lot of graduated-sized boxes to fit inside one another. It is fun and exciting to keep finding smaller boxes inside.

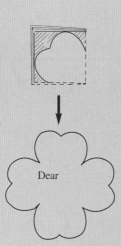

# EASTER

# Bunny A

**Level:** Lower grades
**Time:** 45 minutes
**Materials:** Folding paper: black (6" x 6", or desired size)
Drawing paper (9" x 9")
Scissors, paste and crayons

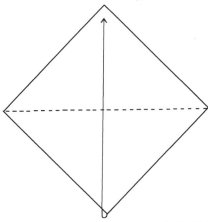

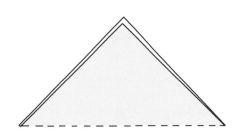

1–2. Fold the paper into a triangle and then open.

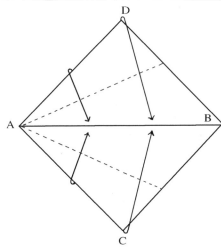

3. Fold sides AC and AD to the center AB line.

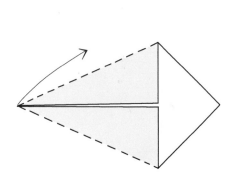

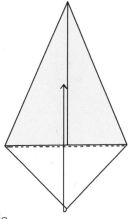

4–5. Turn and fold up the bottom triangle.

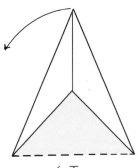

6. Turn.

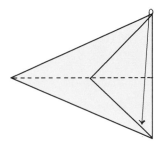

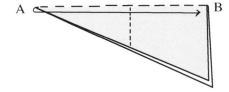

7–8. Fold in half lengthwise.

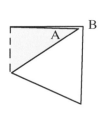

9. Fold point A to B.

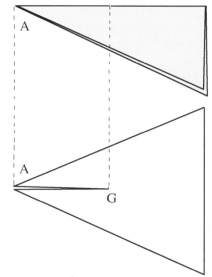

10. Open and cut on the folded line from point A to G.

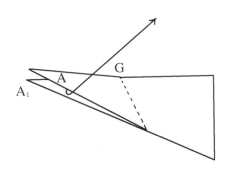

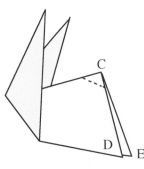

11–12. Fold side A slanting up from the dotted line to form an ear.
Repeat with side A¹, slanting it a bit farther to form the other ear.
See diagram 13. Note: When folding ears, start at G (end of slit).

13. Push down point C a little between D and E.

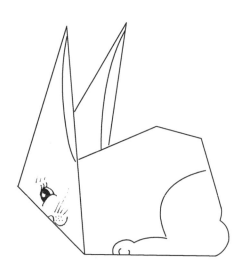

14. Draw the face, ears and hind leg. Round the tail with the scissors. Children can draw a spring picture and paste their bunny on it for the classroom. The bunnies also make nice table decorations.

# Bunny B (Hat)

**Level:** Lower grades
**Time:** 40 minutes
**Materials:** Paper: old newsprint or white newsprint (21 1/2" x 21 1/2")
Crayons, paste and scissors

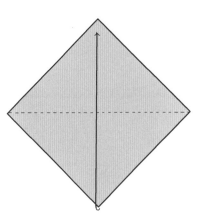

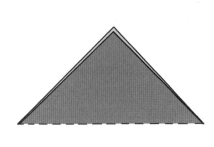

1–2. Fold the paper into a triangle, crease and then unfold.

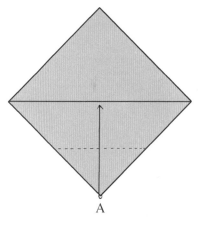

3–4. Fold the bottom point A up to the center of the creased line.

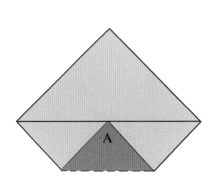

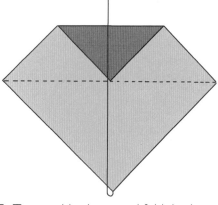

5. Turn upside down and fold the bottom part up on the creased line and press down.

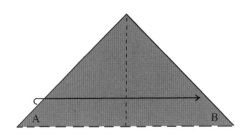

6. Fold in half to make a smaller triangle and then open.

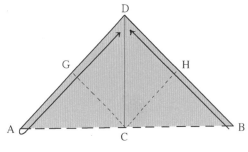

7. Fold sides A and B up on the dotted lines to the top D.

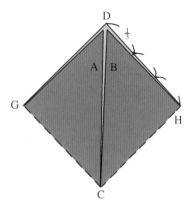

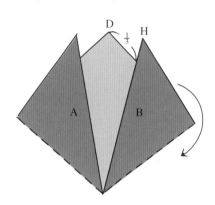

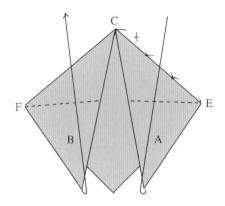

8. Divide and mark off DG and DH into equal thirds.

9. Pull sides A and B down to the first ¹/₃ marks from D.

10. Turn upside-down and mark the CE and CF lines into equal thirds.

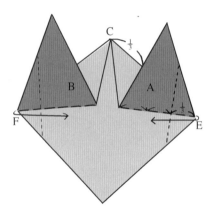

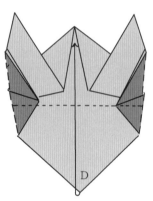

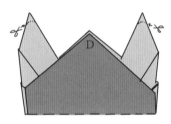

11. Fold parts A and B up on the dotted lines to the first ¹/₃ marks. Fold sides E and F on the dotted lines about ¹/₃ the widths of parts A and B.

12. Fold the bottom D up to the top.

13. Round the ears with scissors.

14. Tuck in the points of the head a little, and paste. Draw the eyes and nose and color the inside of the ears.

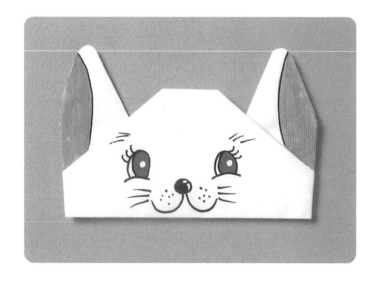

# Bunny C

| | |
|---|---|
| **Level:** | Lower grades and middle grades |
| **Time:** | 1½ or 2 hours |
| **Materials:** | Folding paper: white (8" x 8", or desired size) |
| | Construction paper: white (9" x 12") for bodies of rabbits and for clothes patterns scrap of cloth |
| | Scissors, paste, crayons and scotch tape |

## FINGER PUPPETS

To make the bodies of the finger puppets, trace around the body shapes and then cut them out. Trace the clothes from the patterns. Decorate the clothes with crayons or pieces of colored paper, and paste them on the bodies. To join each body to a bunny head, put paste on the neck and slip it under part F in diagram 12.

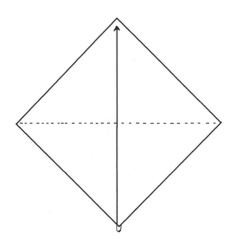

1. Fold in half to make a triangle.

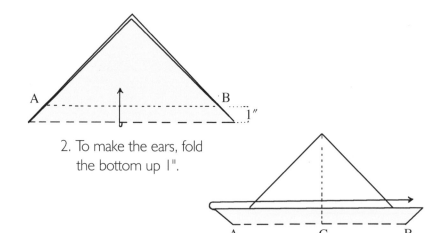

2. To make the ears, fold the bottom up 1".

3. Fold in half again and open.

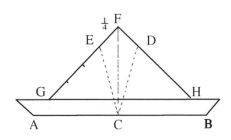

4. Divide and mark GF and HF into fourths.

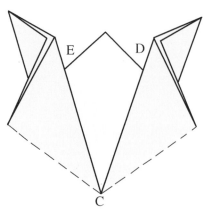

5. Fold the ears AC and BC up along the dotted lines.

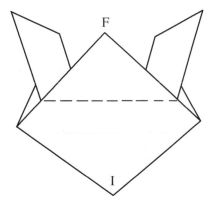

6. Turn over. I is 1" above point C.

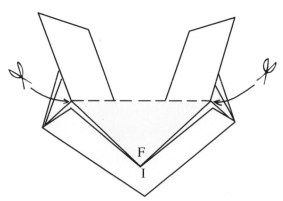

7. Fold F down to I and crease.

42

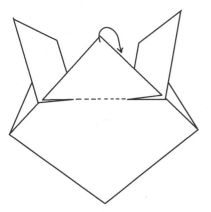

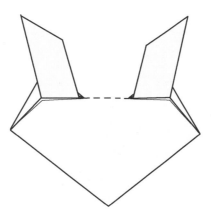

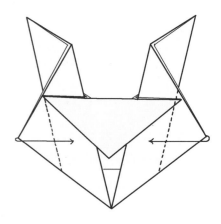

8. Cut in along the creased line the width of the ears. Unfold the triangle.

9. Slip both ears into the slits, and then fold the triangle down over the back.

10. Turn over. Fold both sides on the dotted lines.

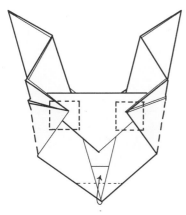

11. Stick two small squares of scotch tape on the dotted line squares.

12. Fold up the bottom point a little to make the face more square.

13. Turn over. Draw the face and ears. When using as a finger puppet, place your finger under F.

April Fun

# Clown's Face

**Level:** Middle grades
**Time:** 50 minutes
**Materials:** Paper: newsprint (10" x 10", or desired size)
Crayons and scissors

1–2. Fold the paper into a triangle and then open.

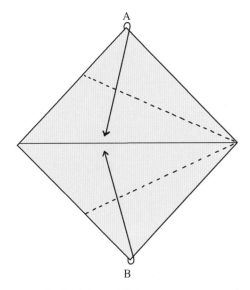

3. Fold A and B to center line. Turn the paper.

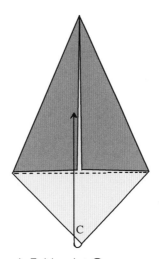

4. Fold point C up on the dotted line.

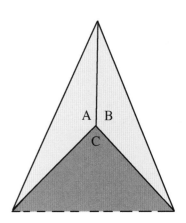

5. Crease each fold.

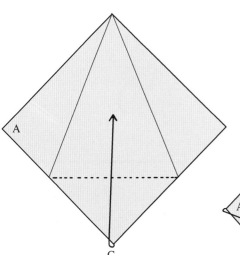

6. Unfold all of the parts.

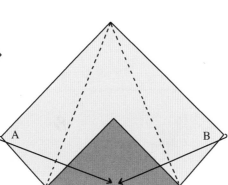

7. Fold up the triangle.

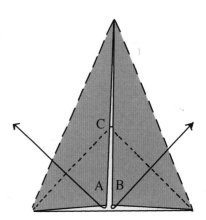

8. Fold A and B over the triangle.

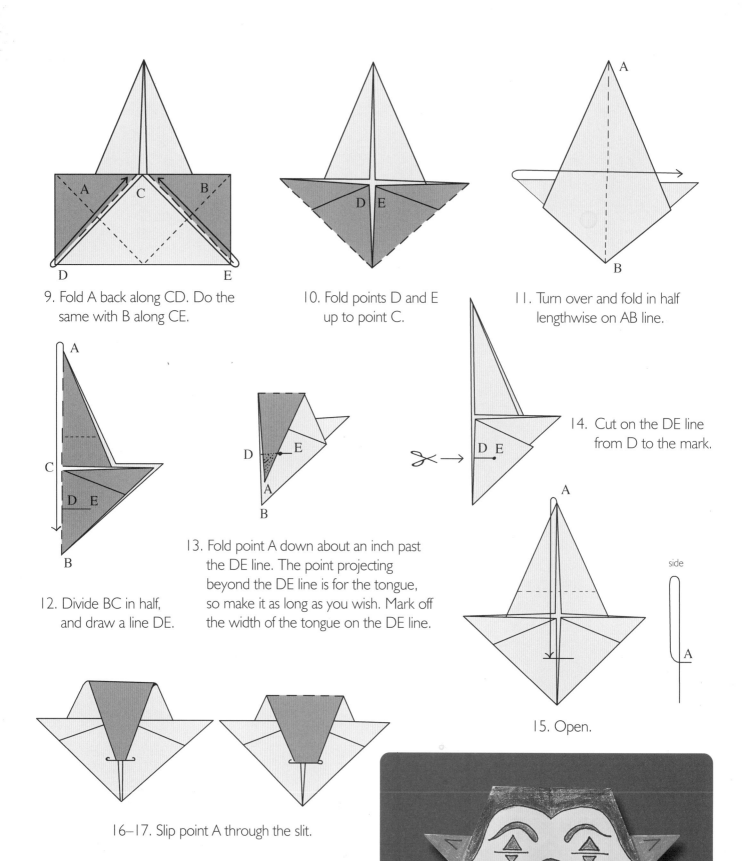

9. Fold A back along CD. Do the same with B along CE.

10. Fold points D and E up to point C.

11. Turn over and fold in half lengthwise on AB line.

12. Divide BC in half, and draw a line DE.

13. Fold point A down about an inch past the DE line. The point projecting beyond the DE line is for the tongue, so make it as long as you wish. Mark off the width of the tongue on the DE line.

14. Cut on the DE line from D to the mark.

15. Open.

side

16–17. Slip point A through the slit.

18. Turn over and press down the tongue so it points downward. Draw any funny face you wish.

# Clown

**Level:** Middle grades
**Time:** 45 minutes
**Materials:** Paper: newsprint (8" x 8", or desired size)
Crayons or water colors and scissors

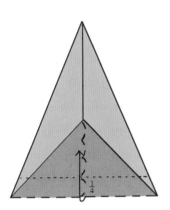

1–5. Follow the steps in diagrams 1–5 of the Clown's Face on page 45.

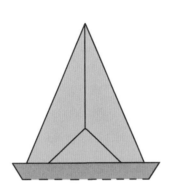

6. Fold up ¼ of the bottom triangle's base.

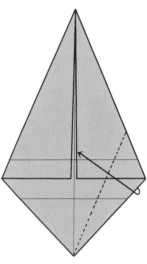

7. Unfold.

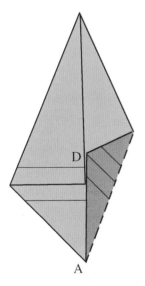

8. Unfold the AD side to the center line and crease well.

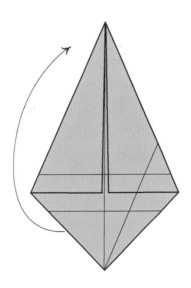

9. Open and turn upside-down.

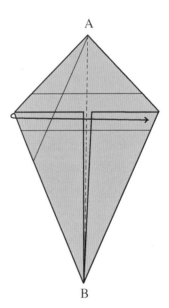

10. Fold in half to the right on the AB line.

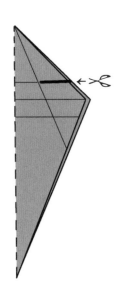

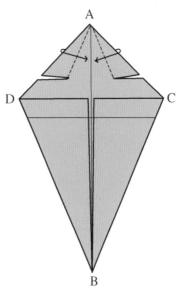

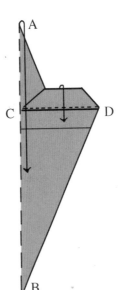

11–12. Cut along the first line from the right side to the slanting line, and then open.

13. Fold parts of AC and AD to the center line.

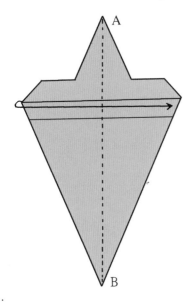

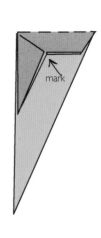

14. Turn over and fold in half lengthwise on the AB line.

15–16. Fold the top part down on the dotted CD line. Make a mark at the corner.

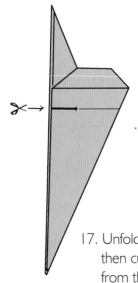

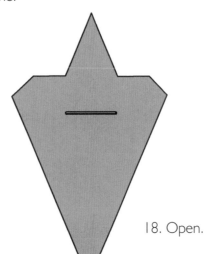

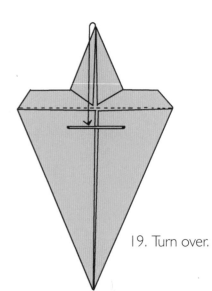

17. Unfold the top part and then cut along the line from the left to the mark.

18. Open.

19. Turn over.

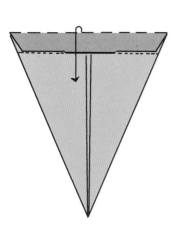

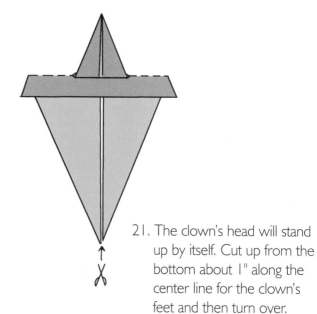

20. Slip point A down and through the slit and pull up carefully.

21. The clown's head will stand up by itself. Cut up from the bottom about 1" along the center line for the clown's feet and then turn over.

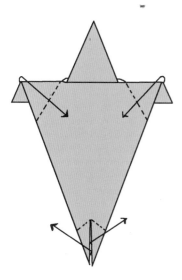

22. Fold the feet out. Fold in the arms.

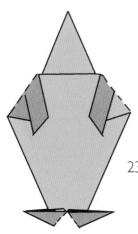

23. Draw the face and color all of the clown with bright colors. You can use this clown as a body for Bunny C on page 41.

# Mother's Day

# Japanese Kimono for Card

**Time:** 45 minutes
**Materials:** Folding paper: printed design (10" x 14")
White paper (3" x 6½") for writing the letter
Scissors, paste and stapler

1. Fold the paper in half lengthwise.

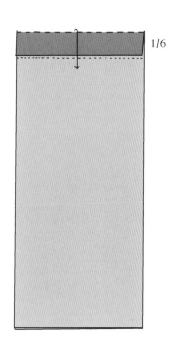

2. Fold the top down ¹⁄₆ the width of AB.

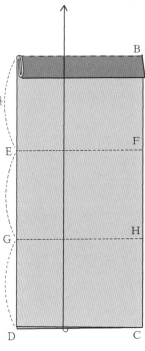

3. Repeat step 2 so you have two folds, each ¹⁄₆ the width of AB.

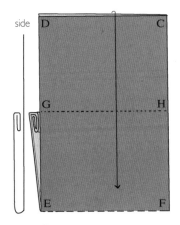

4. Divide BC into three equal parts. Fold the bottom DC part up on the dotted EF line and press down.

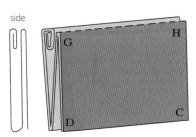

5. Fold the top DC part down on the dotted GH line.

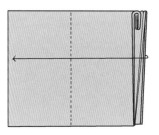

6. Turn over.

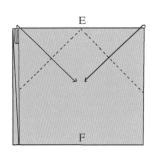

7–8. Fold in half to the left and then open.

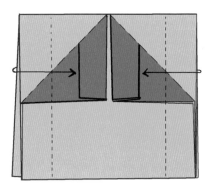

9. Fold the top corners down to the center EF line.

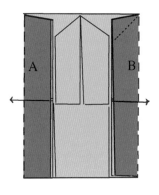

10. Fold both sides on the dotted lines to the collar's edges.

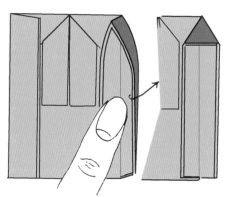

11–13. Spread open parts A and B, and press the tops down into triangles.

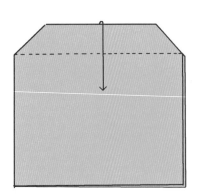
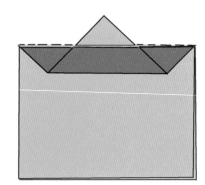

14–15. Turn over and fold the top down on the dotted line.

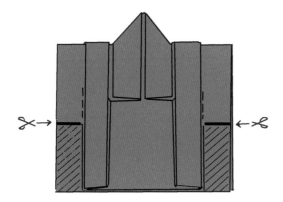

16. Turn over.

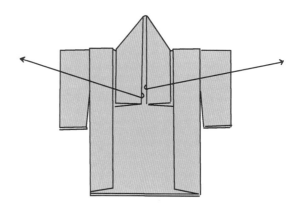

17. Cut out the shaded parts. For a girl's kimono, cut up the dotted lines to make sleeves. The sleeves need not be cut for a boy's kimono.

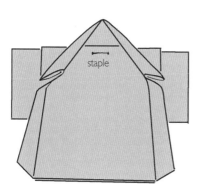

18. Spread the collar open and staple at the top.

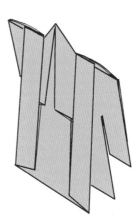

19. Paste the bottom of the sleeves together. The kimono stands by itself by spreading the front and back parts.

## MOTHER'S DAY CARD OR INVITATION CARD

1. Fold the white paper in half. Cut the corners off at the top.

2. Write a greeting on the paper, and slip it inside the kimono..

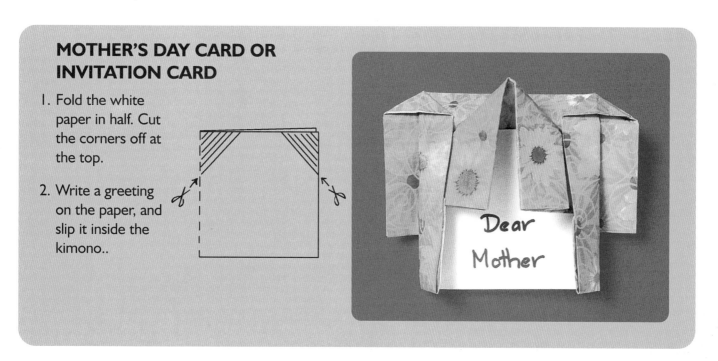

# Carnation for Card

**Level:** Middle grades
**Time:** 45 minutes
**Materials:** Folding paper: red or pink (6" x 6") for the flower
Thin paper: green (5" x 2") for the stem and leaves; white
(8½" x 11½") for writing the letter
Construction paper: blue or purple (9" x 12") for the card
Crayons, scissors and paste

If you are using Japanese origami paper, make sure the colored side of the paper is facing up before folding

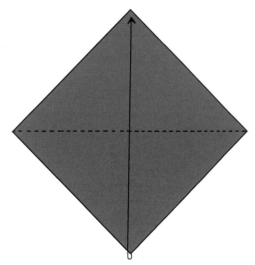

1. Fold the paper into a triangle.

2. Fold again into a smaller triangle. Crease the folded edges well.

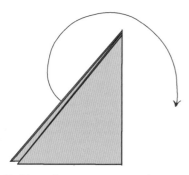

3. Turn the paper around to the right.

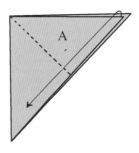

4. Fold part A down on the dotted line and crease well.

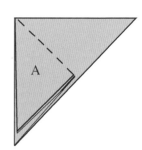

5. Hold A up straight.

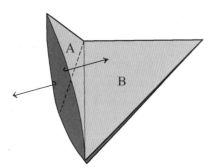

6. Spread open part A to the left and to the right.

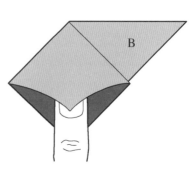

7. Press down into a diamond shape.

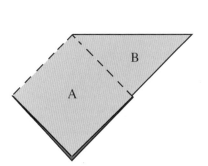

8. Turn over and repeat steps 6–8 with B.

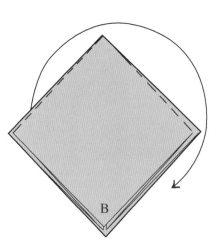

9. Turn it around.

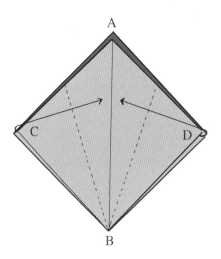

10. Fold the CB and DB sides up along the AB center line.

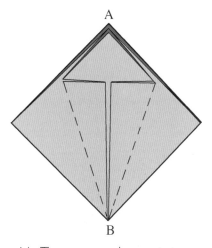

11. Turn over and repeat step 10 with the other side.

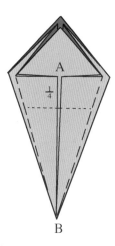

12. Fold the top down on the dotted line $\frac{1}{4}$ the length of the AB line.

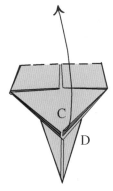

13. Crease the folded part well. Pull part C up and hold part D down.

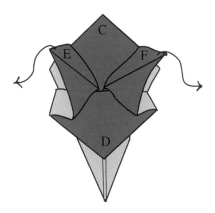

14. Press parts E and F down into diamond shapes.

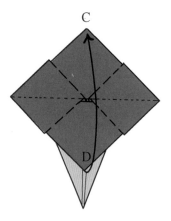
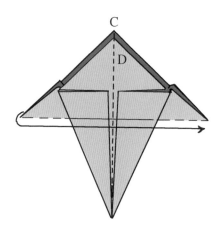
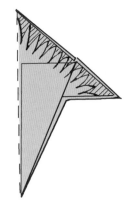

15. Fold the bottom D up on the dotted line to part C.

16. Fold in half to the right.

17. Cut out the shaded parts.

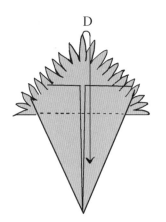

18–19. Open it to the left, and fold the top D part down.

20. Cut out the stem and leaves from the green paper. Paste the stem, flower and leaves on the card.

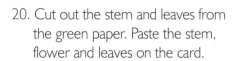

**Materials for Hydrangea:** Folding paper: blue, light blue, purple, lavender or pink (1½" square); green for leaves. Make 25 pieces for each flower and four leaves.

**Materials for Small Flower:** Folding paper: desired color (1½" square for each flower)

**Materials for Morning Glory:** Folding paper: desired color (1¼" or 1½" square for each flower)

## HYDRANGEA

Follow the steps in diagrams 1–11, pages 54–55, for the Carnation.

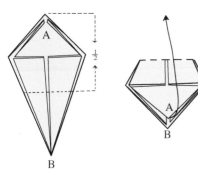 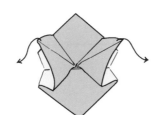 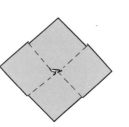

12–15. Fold the top A down to B, and then open.

16. Draw or cut leaves from the green construction paper. Paste the 25 flowers and leaves together as shown in the picture.

## SMALL FLOWER

Follow the same steps as for the Hydrangea. Draw the stem and leaves or cut them from the scraps of thin green paper. Paste the flowers on the stem. Use it for a spring picture or greeting card.

## MORNING GLORY

Follow the steps in diagrams 1–16, pages 54–55, for the Carnation. Draw some curved lines instead of carnation petals, and then open. Cut the stem and leaves out of scraps of green paper. Paste the stem and leaves and the flowers on the paper.

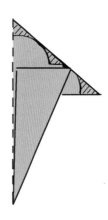

Summer Fun

# Crab

**Level:** Middle and upper grades
**Time:** 40 minutes
**Materials:** Folding paper: orange (3¹/₂" x 3¹/₂", or desired size).
Three pieces are required for one crab.
Scrap of paper for the eyes
Paste, scissors, crayons and a pencil

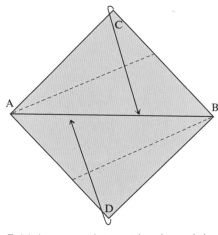

1. Fold the paper into a triangle and then open. Fold parts AC and BD on the dotted lines to the center AB line.

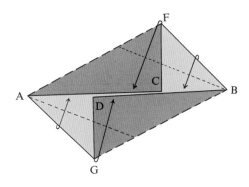

2. Fold the parts AG and BF on the dotted lines to the center AB line. Your paper will be in the shape of a diamond.

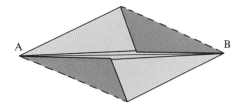

3. Make two more of these diamond shapes. You will need one for the shell and pinchers and two for the body and legs.

## SHELL AND PINCHERS

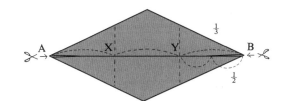

4. Take one of the folded diamond-shaped papers and turn it over. Divide it into equal thirds. Mark the thirds with X and Y on the AB line. Cut in on the center line one half the length of AX and YB.

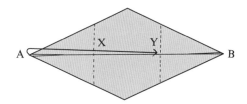

5. Fold point A over Y and crease.

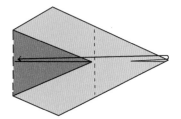 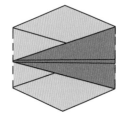 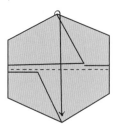 

6–7. Fold point B over to X on top of A. Turn the paper over.

8–9. Fold the paper in half from top to bottom.

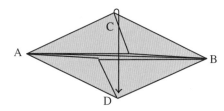

10. Hold part C with your left hand, and gently pull triangle B up with your other hand into the form of the dotted lines. It will look like a pincher. Do the same with triangle A.

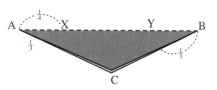

11–12. Draw the eyes on the scrap paper and cut out, then paste them on the head.

## BODY AND LEGS

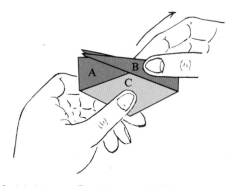

13. Take another of your folded diamond-shaped papers, and fold it in half.

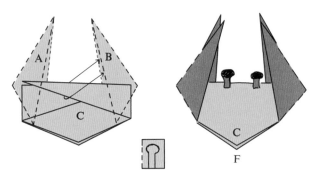

14. Divide into fourths and mark X and Y $\frac{1}{4}$ from the ends of A and B. Divide sides AC and BC into thirds. E and D are $\frac{1}{3}$ marks from A and B. Draw lines to connect EX and YD.

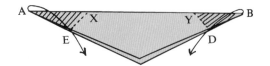 

15–16. Fold the shaded portions of A and B down along the EX and YD lines.

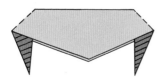

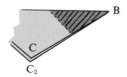 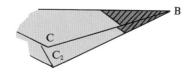

17. Crease the folded parts well, and then open and fold them down on the back side.

18–19. Open parts C and C², and push down the center crease of point B so it folds in between parts C and C². Do the same with point A.

 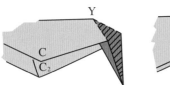

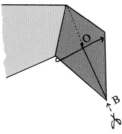 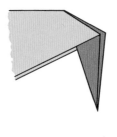

20–21. Crease the dotted lines well, and open part D into a kite shape.

22–23. Cut the center line from point B to the O mark. Close part D. Now you have two legs. Do the same with point A. You now have four legs.

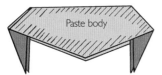

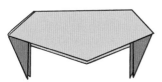

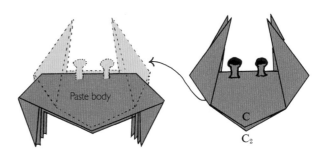

24–25. Take the remaining diamond-shaped paper and repeat steps 13–21. Paste the bodies together.

26–27. Take the shell and pinchers and open the bottom C and C². Put a little paste on the insides. Slip it down on the body. The crab will stand up by itself.

28. Make more crabs using different sized paper to make a crab family. They make a nice aquarium.

# Ship A

**Level:** Lower grades
**Time:** 50 minutes
**Materials:** Folding paper: white (7" x 7")
Drawing paper: white or blue (12" x 9")
Color crayons or water paint
Paste

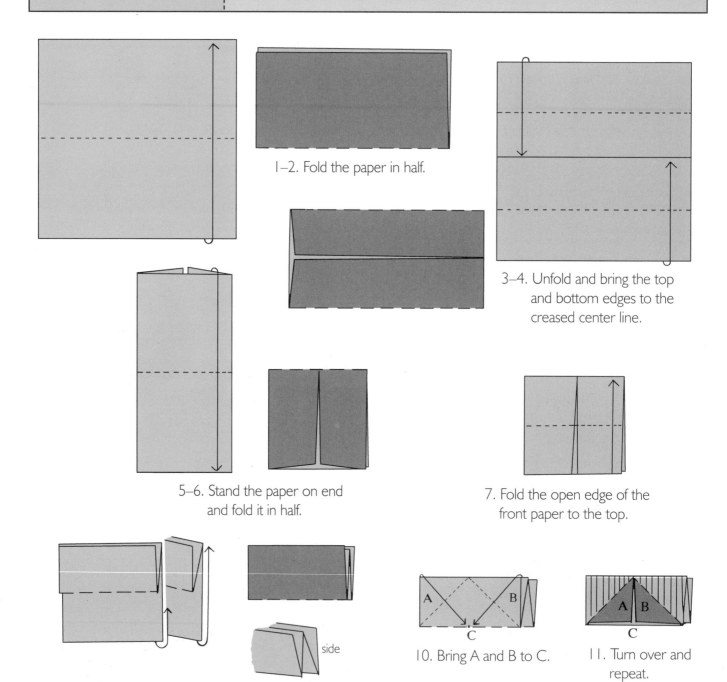

1–2. Fold the paper in half.

3–4. Unfold and bring the top and bottom edges to the creased center line.

5–6. Stand the paper on end and fold it in half.

7. Fold the open edge of the front paper to the top.

8–9. Turn the paper over and repeat.

side

10. Bring A and B to C.

11. Turn over and repeat.

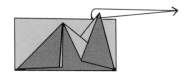

12. Pull the top layer of the folded-in flap out to the right.

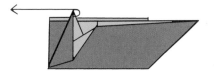

13–14. Do the same to the left side.

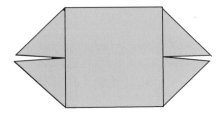

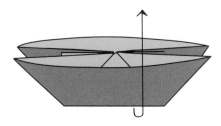

15. Turn the paper and repeat. It will look like this.

16. Open the bottom of the boat.

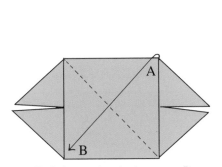

17. Bring point A down to B.

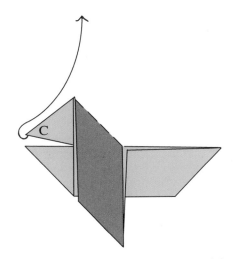

18. Bring point C so that it points straight up and the left flap unfolds.

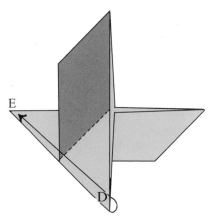

19. Bring point D over to E.

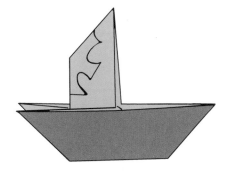

20. Draw the ship's mark on the sail and color the body of the ship. Paint ocean scenery and paste the ship on it.

## Ship B

**Level:** Middle grades
**Time:** 1 hour
**Materials:** Folding paper: white (7" x 7")
Drawing paper: white or blue (12" x 9")
Color crayons or water paint
Scissors and paste

Follow diagrams 1–3
for Ship A, page 62.

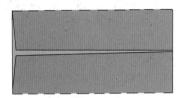

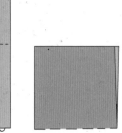

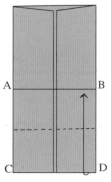

4. Bring the top and bottom edges to the center line.

5–6. Stand the paper on end and fold it in half.

7–8. Unfold and bring the CD edge up to the AB line.

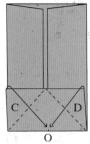

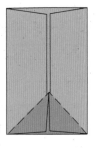

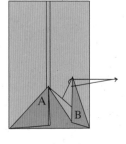

9–10. Bring C and D, which you folded, down to point O.

11. Pull the top layer of the folded-in flap B out to the right. Repeat with flap A.

12–13. Cut left and right above the hull along the front, cutting only a single layer of paper.

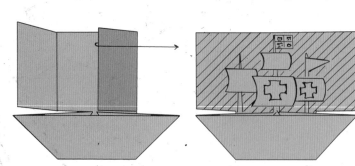

14. Draw the sails, masts and flags. Cut out as neccessary. Paint the ocean scenery and paste the ship on it.